This Book Belongs to

_____

Date I received this book

_____

31 DAYS OF CONSISTENCY WITH THE LORD!

A DEVOTIONAL

Written By: Whitley Witcher

I dedicate this book to the Lord, as He has opened my eyes to the truth that being consistent with Him is the greatest thing in life. Without Him, I can do nothing. He is the one who unlocks doors that no man can shut. He's the one who is worth falling in love with.

Hello, my name is Whitley, and I have been praying that this devotional book would reach you. You are a miracle, and I see a great purpose in you. You have been trying to find ways to get closer to the Lord and not knowing what to do. I'm so glad you have decided to take the time to stop and pick this up. It's time to let the Lord take control of the wheel. You have been driving for too long, and now it's time to stop. Don't worry about the steps ahead. You're making the best decision of your life by choosing to be consistent with the Lord.

Are you willing to sacrifice something to get close the LORD….

You can do it…..

It's just you and the LORD...

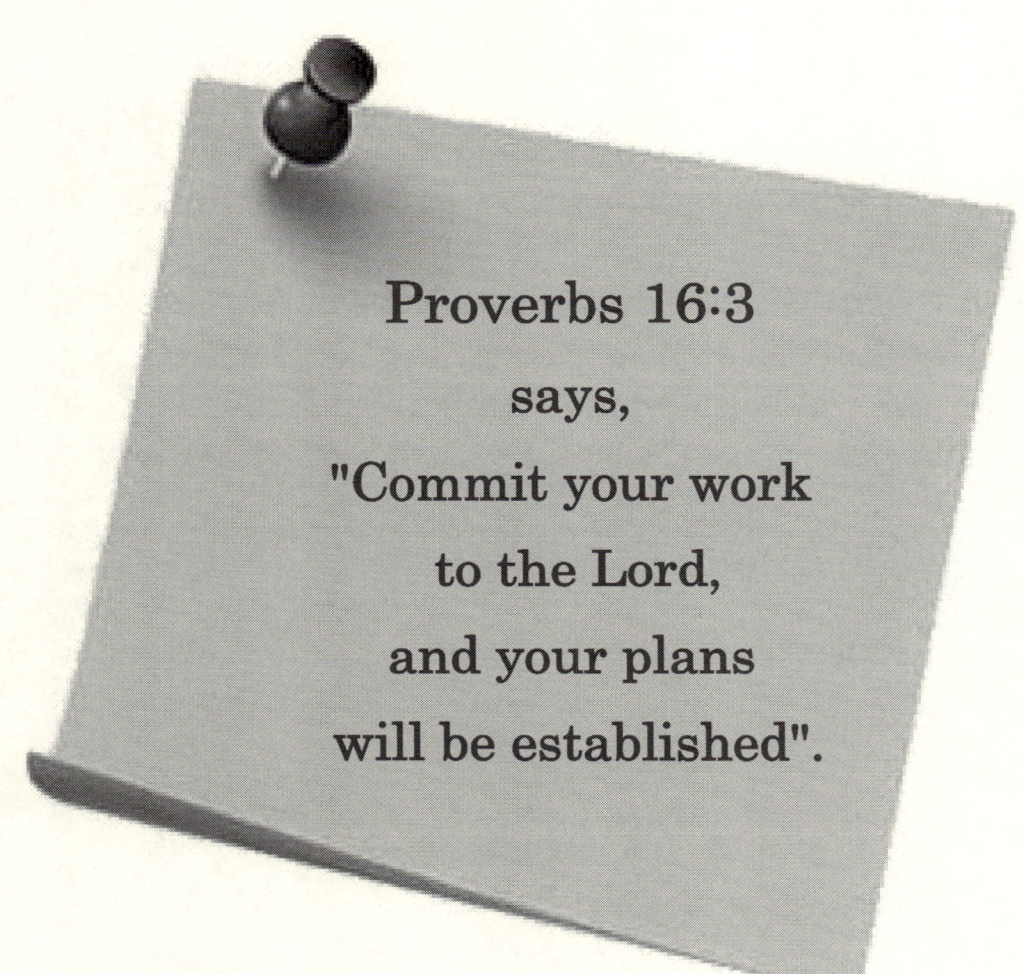

consistency

noun
> **conformity in the application of something, typically that which is necessary for the sake of logic, accuracy, or fairness.**

God woke me up one morning and told me to pray. As I woke up, I remember telling God, how tired I was. So, I went back to sleep. We all know when God wakes you up at 3am in the morning, He's trying to get your attention. I remember waking back up and hearing Him say, how much do you truly love me. I said I love you so much, you are more than enough. He said I need more consistency. The LORD said, I am CONSISTENT in everything that I do. Haven't I always been there for you. I'm the Parent that will never leave you even after death. I said, Yes LORD you have, and you are everything that I need. I begin to weep and thank God for being there and never leaving myside. I begin to pray. As the morning went on, I got in my car, I heard God say the word Consistency. I heard it a few times. I wrote it down and went on with my day. Later that day after church a friend of mines called, and we began to talk about relationships. I begin to hear the word Consistency again. The Lord said, "That is what I want from you." When I got home the LORD started speaking. He said, "I want you to do a 31 day of CONSISTENCY with me." I begin writing. The LORD said it's not just for you, but I am calling my children to spend time with me. It's in our alone time that we begin to see how the LORD wants to grow and use us.

Consistency comes with time, patients, and being steady in the word of God. As we all know in a relationship, we require our mate to be consistent. We want them to put forth the effort of being Faithful. Why not take the same energy and put that in with the only one worth it all, our savior Jesus Christ. The Lord wants us to dive deeper into Him daily. I can honestly say I didn't always strive with consistency. God had to open my eyes and show me that there was more to Him. He showed me a newborn baby. As I saw the baby it wanted more food. The more you feed the baby the more the baby grows. So, the more we allow God to feed us the more we grow in Him. We become older & wiser.

For the next 31 days I pray you take the steps and allow God to grow you in your walk with Him. When it's over I pray that you continue to allow Jesus to come in and have His way in your heart and life. Let this Encourage you. Our Journey with God is everyday not just some days.

Content

C
    Choose
    Change
    Commitment

O
    Obey
    Open
    Oil

N
    Navigate
    Necessary
    Noise

S
    Shelter
    Study
    Sure

I
    Injection
    Intimacy
    Increase

S
    Sorry
    Supply

T
    Transformation
    Test
    Testify

E
    Effort
    Elevation
    Early

N
    New
    Nourishment

C
    Challenge
    Company
    Cover

Y
    Yield
    Years
    You

Remember the Lord loves you.

John 3:16: "For God so loved the world that He gave His only Son, that whoever believes in Him should not perish but have eternal life"

Romans 8:35–39: God's love is stronger than death, famine, persecution, and other difficulties

Romans 5:8: "God has demonstrated His love toward us—He has proved His love toward us—in that while we were still sinners, Christ died for us"

1 Corinthians 13:4-7: God's love is patient, kind, and never gives up

1 John 4:18: Perfect love expels all fear.

Day 1

Choose

**Even in our strongest moments we become weak,
but we must choose the RIGHT door.**

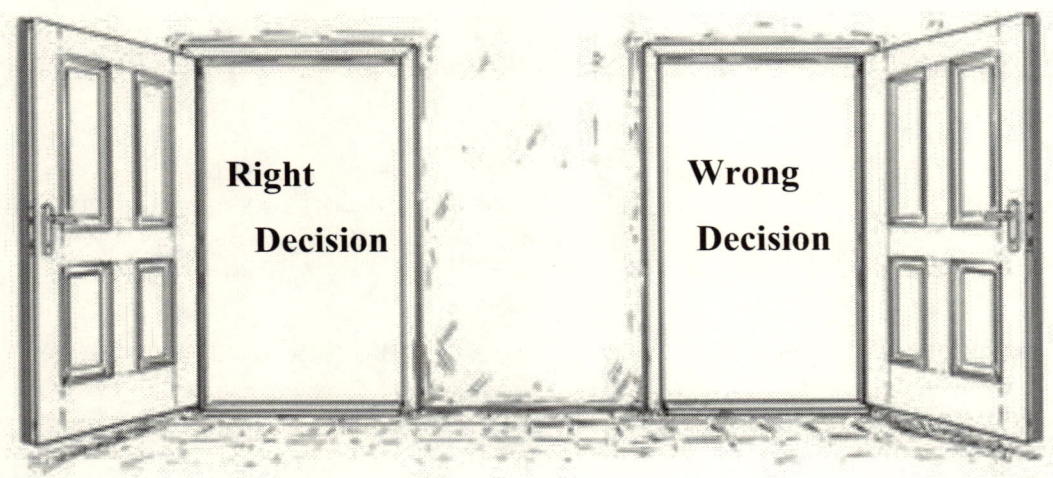

What Will You CHOOSE?

Who are you choosing to Serve? When we choose something, we can use so many words such as pick out, prefer, wish, desire, select… the list can go on and on. In the end we still recognize that we have the choice to choose. When choosing a team, we want the best. No one likes picking the weakest link. No matter if it's in school, on our jobs, sports, or just simply for fun. We choose the strongest of them all. We want the one that will help us win. Have you chosen the right person? Something to think about…

Really look at your life. Who is leading you? We must start by recognizing who oversees our life. The Lord loves us so much that He wants us to continue to bless us. The Lord said He wants to start in you. We are never too young or too old to stop growing in the LORD. The first thing I said was Lord, I choose you. He said, "No you choose me when you think I'm needed." I began to cry. I felt the pain. He showed me times where I chose Family, Friends, Shopping, and even Mates over Him. He said don't you know I am the bread of life. I am everything that you need.

John 14:6 NIV Jesus answered, 'I am the way the truth and the light. No one comes to the father except through me.

Joshua 24:15 NIV But if serving the LORD **seems undesirable to you, then choose for yourselves this day whom you will serve, whether the gods your ancestors served beyond the Euphrates, or the gods of the Amorites, in whose land you are living. But as for me and my household, we will serve the L**ORD**."**

So again, the LORD said who will you choose. When life happens some of us walk out on Him. We give up because it becomes too much for us to handle. No one likes losing control of the wheel when driving. Instead of being in control why don't we give to the one who is in control of it all. He's the best driver that will never wreck. Deciding doesn't mean that your life will be golden. You are simply saying Jesus I trust you with my life.

Let's Pray… Lord, forgive me for choosing material things over you. Lord come into my heart and clean me up. Help me to make the right decisions when it comes to serving you. Lord, from this day forward I choose to walk and talk with you. I choose to do things in Faith and be honest. Lord when I feel like I'm weak continue to guide me in your word. Help me to see daily why choosing you is the right choice. Thank you, LORD, for opening up my eyes, in Jesus' name Amen!

Day 2

CHANGE!!!

Have you changed your attire in the Lord?

Or are you still serving in yesterday clothing.

Change requires a new wardrobe…

Change can seem hard when you are use to your old ways. When you look at the word Change what do you really see? Some of us can say we have change and still changing but when God looks at our heart we are still in the same position as we were a few years ago. Change means: make (someone or something) different; alter or modify, or to replace (something) with something else, especially something of the same kind that is newer or better; substitute one thing for (another).

When it comes to shopping many of us like buying new things. I must admit I love clothes. Most of us try to buy things that no one has. The question is: What happens when we look like everyone else. On the outside we are looking like everyone. When we begin to do things like the world. Let's begin a clean slate by taking off the things of the world and put on the righteousness of the LORD. Your outer appearance looks better when you are yourself.

Have you looked at your attire. What are you representing that shows that a change has come about. Many times, in life when we lose weight, we notice the change. One of the biggest steps is taking off our heavy clothes and getting ones that fit. No one likes to walk around in heavy attire. God wants us to take off the things that are heavy in our life and lay it at his feet. That's where consistency comes back in. We must maintain change. The more you take off the more God can use you. Let the layers of lies, manipulation, money, sex and so much more. Drop it all off at the Lord's feet.

2 Corinthians 5:17 KJV   Therefore, if any man be in Christ, he is a new creature: old things are passed away; behold, all things are become new.

Jeremiah 29:11 For I know the thoughts that I think toward you, saith the Lord, thoughts of peace, and not of evil, to give you an expected end.

Prayer…

Lord we just simply say thank you! Thank you for showing us our attire. Help us to take off the things that's not of you. Help us to be better in our appearance. Lord open up our eyes to show us that we can be ourselves. Lord let us see how you see us. Forgive us of our sins. Lord thank you for Change in Jesus name Amen!

Day 3

Once you **Choose** Him
you **Change** your attire for Him.
To now **COMMIT** to His will…

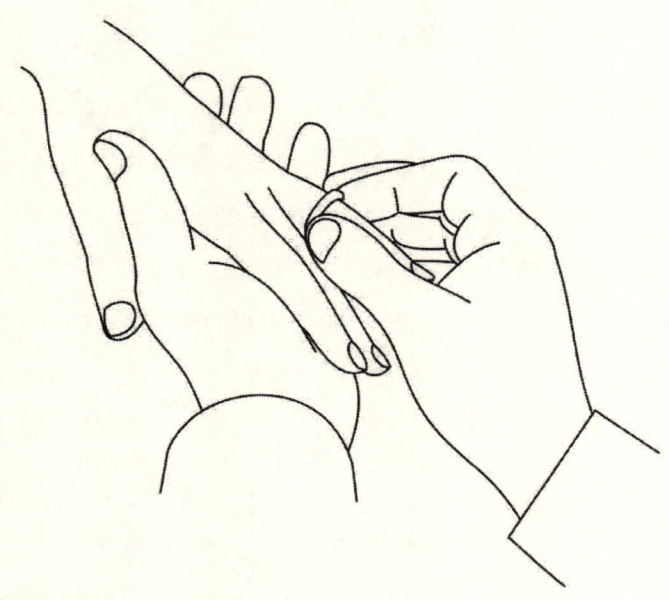

Are you ready to say, I do? Many of us are afraid when it comes to making decisions. Simply because we feel like we are going to be let down. So many of us have faced rejection that it causes us to reject the one who is the provider. I know marriage is not meant for everyone but in the spiritual side God is at the alter waiting on us to make up our mind will we marry Him. To be married comes with hard work. It says to marry for better or worse through sickness and health. The good part about this is the LORD is simply everything. He will always be there. Even when we make it to heaven. We don't have to worry about Him leaving us because He was there from the start. He comforts, heals, provides, and most of all He loves us Unconditionally. Who wouldn't want to be married to the best.

I must say when the LORD gave me this, I was in a Committed relationship, but I wasn't faithful. There were times when I would lean on others instead of HIM. There were times when I wasn't being consisted in our alone times, Commitment is a big step when you agree to something. The question is are you ready to commit to the one who is in control of it all. Just know you are making the best decision when you step at the altar.

There's not a time where in a relationship we don't have up's and down's. We all face days when we say; I give up… This not for me… or I don't want to be committed to this anymore. Just seem like we are burden down with life. The blessing of it all is when you make the vow to God. He is right there. We can't see Him, but you must trust and know that He is there to carry the load. He wants to be the person that will solve it all. He's just that good.

Psalm 37:5 Commit your way to the LORD; trust in him, and he will act.

Revelation 19: 7-9 ⁷ Let us be glad and rejoice, and give honour to him: for the marriage of the Lamb is come, and his wife hath made herself ready. ⁸ And to her was granted that she should be arrayed in fine linen, clean and white: for the fine linen is the righteousness of saints. ⁹ And he saith unto me, Write, Blessed *are* they which are called unto the marriage supper of the Lamb. And he saith unto me, These are the true sayings of God.

Prayer

Hallelujah, to the best example of a Husband. Lord we just say thank you. Lord, we commit ourselves to your will and to your ways. We thank you that you haven't gave up on us. You met me at the altar with my brokenness, my flaws and all. Thank you for cleaning us up. Thank you for loving us the right way so that we can love others in Jesus name Amen.

Day 4

Are WE Obeying the LORD? Why is it so hard to obey the LORD? You may say it is easy but just look back over your life, have you always obeyed your parents. As children growing up most of us were good and some were just disobedient. Many of us have a hard time following instructions. How often when you were told to do something you didn't. I was a good student in school, but I talked to my friends too much. That would always get me in trouble. So, around report card time I had a N in conduct because I wouldn't stop talking sometimes. I didn't benefit from getting rewards from my mother. Begin to look at this in an older way. When your boss tells you to do something, some of us are lazy or just didn't obey. We then get penalized for not following directions. It doesn't feel good to be punished. How often did you lose out on things because of your disobedience?

The definition of Obey is to comply with the command, direction, or request of (a person or a law); submit to the authority of. Look at this in a spiritual way. Many of us seem to disobey because of distractions. We tend to let other things get in the way that we lose focus of the path to take. How many times will you keep allowing yourself to drop the ball. We must get on track to do what's right. Even if that means cutting some people and places off.

If we took the word obey and use the letters backwards. We will see that the first step is to say **Y**es to the LORD's will. He will **E**levate us higher so we can reap the good **B**enefits that will make room for many **O**pportunities. The LORD blessings never run out, but we can stop our own blessings by not obeying the instructor. Who is our instructor? If you have given your life over to the world than you have the wrong teacher. The Lord is jealous.

Exodus 34:14 NKJV (for you shall worship no other god, for the LORD, whose name is Jealous, is a jealous God)

Deuteronomy 27:10 Therefore you shall obey the voice of the LORD your God, and observe His commandments and His statutes which I command you today.

Prayer

Lord, we want to stop and ask for forgiveness for not obeying you. Lord, we ask that you forgive us for putting other things in the way. We want to ask that you help us to get on track and make a **Yes** with our heart and not just with our mouth. That we want you to erase our failure and help us so we can **Elevate** in your word to reap the **Benefits** so that many doors of **Opportunity** will show up in Jesus name Amen

Day 5

OPEN your Heart to the LORD

Today is the day to Open up to God? One of the hardest things to do is to be open to someone who will stab you in the back. Most of us can say we don't like to be open about our issues. We become afraid of everyone knowing our business. It feels like you wasted too much of your time feeding the wrong person food. They eat up all your dirty laundry, money, secrets just to spill it out to someone else. Most of the time when they cut you with a knife you try to hurt them back. Let me just say that is not the way to be. Although some people are not to be trusted, everyone is not like that. When you think about all the times you've poured your heart out about personal things, and the person you were talking to had things on their mind that they weren't really listening to you. Then you get upset and become hurt. We all can say we have been there. I have found someone who I can say, If they can hold the whole world then you know your secrets are safe. He's the best mentor, father, everything you need him to be. His name is JESUS. He will sit and listen. I have learned that talking to the LORD was the best decision I have ever made in my life. All my crying, dark days, and even all my sins, He was there. He wiped every tear, turned my dark days to better days and washed all my sins away. Who else do you know that can do that? NO ONE…. You must learn how to open to the LORD. Talk to Him like you talk to your family and friends. Time with the LORD will strengthen you in so many ways. You cannot find a friend like the lowly JESUS no matter how you try.

When we are certain that the LORD loves us, is interested in us, and has a plan for our lives, our focus will shift from what we or other people think to what He thinks. We can open our hearts up to him by listening, talking, turning, and committing to being close to him.

1 Samuel 16:7 "But the Lord said unto Samuel, look not on his countenance, or on the height of his stature; because I have refused him: for the Lord seeth not as man seeth; for man looketh on the outward appearance, but the Lord looketh on the heart."

Psalm 62:8 "Trust in him at all times; ye people, pour out your heart before him: God is a refuge for us. Selah"

No matter what we go through Trust and know that God will help us through it. We just must open our heart to Him. He will never let us down. I'm a true witness of that. Whatever you done God will heal and forgive.

Prayer
Dear Heavenly Father forgive me for not trusting you with my life. Help me to lean on you and not others. Continue to show me my heart and fix me. Lord, I am going to take this day forward and come to you with my problems. Lord I just want to say thank you for not telling others my secrets and not counting me out when others have, in Jesus name Amen.

Day 6

ARE YOU READY FOR THE OIL…

Are you chasing after the right Oil?

As we know, many of us love oil. We use it in so many ways. Let's start in the kitchen, it is a must have ingredient. Especially when we are frying chicken. The oil must be good and hot to be able to fry chicken in it. If the oil is not good you can taste it in the chicken. You also can smell when its burning. No one likes eating burnt chicken. Even when it comes to baking cakes if we miss putting oil in the cake it doesn't turn out right. It is necessary. We even use it when we are doing hair, making sure our scalp is nice and oily. Not only that but some of us use it for our bodies to make our skin soft and shiny. We even use oil for our cars. Every 3,000 miles you know it's time to get a oil change. So, as we see Oil is necessary for our daily life. Can't live without it. There are different types of oil, that many of us experience on some have made us break out and some have helped in so many ways.

We looked at the Natural, let us see it from a Spiritual side. Oil represents this presence and power of the Spirit of God throughout the Bible. Jesus was often referred to as the Anointed One. Oil symbolizes wealth, abundance, health, energy, and is a vital ingredient for a good life. When God called Aaron to be the first priest of Israel, he was anointed with oil as a symbol of being consecrated to God for this holy work. In **Exodus 30:30-32**, a special oil was mixed that God said should be used to anoint Aaron and his sons and remain set aside only for this purpose. "Anoint Aaron and his sons and consecrate them so they may serve me as priests. Say to the Israelites, 'This is to be my sacred anointing oil for the generations to come. Do not pour it on anyone else's body and do not make any other oil using the same formula. It is sacred, and you are to consider it sacred. Oil was also used when Samuel anointed David to be the first king of Israel. In **1 Samuel 16:13,** it says: "So Samuel took the horn of oil and anointed him in the presence of his brothers, and from that day on the Spirit of the LORD came powerfully upon David." Scriptures also make mention of oil as associated with healing, offerings to God, and unity. When Jesus sent the disciples out in healing ministry, **Mark 6:12-13** says they anointed people with oil. They went out and preached that people should repent. They drove out many demons and anointed many sick people with oil and healed them." Oil was used as an offering to God, in part because oil was required to keep the lamp continuously burning inside the temple. The continuously burning lamp inside the tabernacle represented the Spirit of God continuously dwelling among His people. Oil also is spoken of as a uniting element in **Psalm 133:1-2**, which says: "Behold, how good and pleasant it is when brothers dwell in unity. It is like the precious oil on the head, running down on the beard, on the beard of Aaron, running down on the collar of his robes!" When Christians act unified, they represent how the Holy Spirit can bring an eclectic, unique, diverse group of people together as one in Christ.

Ask yourself this question, have you been anointed with the right oil? As we all know you can't allow any one to Anoint you. Just like everyone can't pray over you. Ask the LORD to guide you. If you need healing or to get ready to step in your calling pray that your leader can anoint you.

Prayer

Lord, we simply say thank you for the oil. We know that in our daily lives we use oil for many things. In our spiritual walk Lord, we ask that you continue to anoint us in your word. Lord many are sick in their body we ask that you anoint them with healing, not only in our body but also in our mind. Free us from things of the world. LORD, we ask that you not stop anoint our hands to be able to do your will. Not our will but your will. Pour the oil on us God that we may live the way you want us to live. Thank you, in Jesus name Amen.

Day 7

Who's Navigation are you Following?

Which way is the Lord leading you?
The Lord leads everyone in a different direction.

I must start off by saying following the navigation in today's time seem like its easy… right. Well, what happens when it leads you to the middle of nowhere? It becomes a little scary, at least for me. I can't speak for anybody else. Sometimes it causes headaches, anxiety, maybe even panic attacks. When Ubering I used to panic when I got to my destination of dropping them off, the scariest part was finding my way back. One day the Navigation wasn't picking up and I was in a scary place with no stores nearby and pretty much nothing but land. My internet on my phone went out. Talking about panic… After Panicking I had to pray. I know you maybe saying you should have done that in the beginning. Well, being honest I didn't I had to trust God to lead me to the main road. Following the holy spirit is how I made it out. I could have panic out in the middle of nowhere if I didn't Trust the LORD's navigation. I get teary eyed because that's all He wants us to trust in His guidance.

Navigation not only in which way to go but also how we go through things such as; jobs, finance, relationships, & children. Navigation requires a plan. God has a plan and purpose for our life that contains a future and hope found in Jesus Christ. We must decide this is the best direction for our life and determine to follow His Way.

Proverbs 3:6 In all thy ways acknowledge him, and he shall direct thy paths. (NKJV)

Proverbs 16:9 A man's heart deviseth his way: but the LORD directeth his steps. (NKJV)

Isaiah 48:17 Thus says the LORD, your Redeemer, The Holy One of Israel: "I *am* the LORD your God, who teaches you to profit, who leads you by the way you should go. (NKJV)

Isaiah 43:19 Behold, I will do a new thing, now it shall spring forth; shall you not know it? I will even make a road in the wilderness *and* rivers in the desert. (NKJV)

So just know whatever direction you go make sure you follow the right Navigation. Following Christ was the best decision that I made. He led me in a place no one else could. Never stop following the LORD. As we all know, to survive we must have a plan. Have a plan on what job to decide to take, who to marry, or date etc.

Prayer

Lord, we stop to say thank you for being our compass. Continue to lead us in the right direction. When we want to follow another map helps us to stay focus on you. Be our light in the dark tunnel. Lord, help us through our daily life. If there is someone struggling with following your steps Lord I pray that they see that you are the end of the road. You are our way up and our way down. You are omnipresent. You can move North, South, East & West. Thank you for being there when I didn't know which way to go. I love you just because I can trust you to never let me down. Forgive me for making the wrong turn. Thank you for helping me get back on track in Jesus name, Amen.

Day 8

CUT IT OFF

You are NECESSARY! Stop allowing others to tell you it's unnecessary for the changes you made to better you? Many times, in life people say harsh words that lead us to think that we are not needed. Think about when you were in school, it was necessary to go because they would say we need our education. Education is necessary to survive in life. Many of us gave up on it because we listen to others say it wasn't necessary. Or how about thinking when you are cooking and someone says you don't need to add sugar, or maybe even salt. We begin to say it is necessary. It can be one of the main ingredients that you need to get a good outcome. How about when you are faced with a challenging situation. You do what is necessary for you and the family. It can be hard to decide on things that can easily take your focus off the solution. When it's a problem you can't just walk away from it because it always comes back up. You must work it out. I have prayed myself out a lot of situations. Simply because it was necessary for my health and to have peace of mind.

Let's begin to dive deeper into the word Necessary it means essential, indispensable, requisite indicate something vital for the fulfillment of a need. Necessary applies to something without which a condition cannot be fulfilled or to an inevitable consequence of certain events, conditions, etc.: Food is necessary to life, also the word of God. It's how we get through this world we live in. Some think it is unnecessary to have it. If you read **Psalms 119:11 NLT "I have hidden your word in my heart, that I might not sin against you."** We must study it, read it, pray over it. They say you can't live without air. Well, we really can't live without Him (GOD). **Psalms 139 14 I will praise thee; for I am fearfully and wonderfully made: marvellous are thy works; and that my soul knoweth right well. 15 My substance was not hid from thee, when I was made in secret, and curiously wrought in the lowest parts of the earth.**

If you are trying to stay on the right track necessary has to be a rule in your book. I simply want to stop and encourage you to keep staying on track. You will make it out better than you was going in. You know why because you are necessary for the Job. The assignment that God has for you is waiting for you to pick it up. Don't worry about what others are saying. You just make sure you show up. Show up for all what God has for you. You will win my sister and brother.

PRAYER

Lord, we say thank you for changing our minds from unnecessary to necessary. Thank you for giving us the job. We thank you for the keys. A time such as this you allowed us to show up at the right place and time. God forgive us for putting ourselves down. Help us to stay on track. Thank you for letting us make it to the finish line. We block out any distractions. We rebuke the negative people in our ears. God continue to give us strength for each assignment that we have been called to in JESUS, name AMEN!!!

Day 9

There is too much NOISE

and YOU can't hear...

Silence the NOISE I love listening to music. I mean I have it so loud I tune everything around me out. I block distractions from coming in at least that's what I thought. When my child walks in the room tapping me on my shoulder became a distraction. Or if I'm outside on the porch enjoying the quietness and someone starts arguing, maybe even the sound of a car wreck or the ambulance passing by. It becomes a distraction to me. Your story maybe you in your house and its peaceful there until your spouse comes in arguing and then its like they broke the quietness. Now your heart is beating fast, and you are disturbed. Your mind seems to be going everywhere. Have you ever screamed out loud BE QUIET?

As we see our life can be busy with many different sounds around. Have God ever tried to talk to you but because the noise you couldn't hear Him. Do you have the volume so loud that you can't hear the voice of the LORD? Maybe you don't think so…. You may be like oh I know the voice of the LORD, but have you ever wondered it could even be the devil. Well stop and pray and see does your mind stays focused or do it drift away to other things. We must learn how to pray for the noise around us, also to allow the Lord to speak to us. All God wants is silence when we come to Him. He wants our minds to be clear. Just as if a friend called and said I need to talk to you. We give them our undivided attention. Let's give God that. He is not looking for perfection but a willing vessel. He knows everything so all you need is to kill the things around you to give the LORD His time.

Amos 5: 21-24 MSG 21 "I can't stand your religious meetings. I'm fed up with your conferences and conventions. 22 I want nothing to do with your religion projects, your pretentious slogans and goals. I'm sick of your fund-raising schemes, your public relations and image making. 23 I've had all I can take of your noisy ego-music. When was the last time you sang to me? 24 Do you know what I want? I want justice - oceans of it. I want fairness - rivers of it. That's what I want. That's all I want.

Matthew 9:23 Jesus came to the ⌐ synagogue ⌐ leader's house. He saw flute players and a noisy crowd. 24 He said to them, "Leave! The girl is not dead. She's sleeping." But they laughed at him. 25 When the crowd had been put outside, Jesus went in, took her hand, and the girl came back to life.

PRAYER Lord, thank you for showing us sounds that's a distraction to you. Forgive us for the sound. We know you are perfect in all your ways. Help us this day forward to silence the Noise around us in Jesus name Amen.

Day 10 Shelter

Protection through the storm…….

The Lord is my Shelter…

Everyone needs Shelter. As children growing up our parents were our shelter. They knew how to protect us. No matter if it was a dog running after us. They knew how to keep us from getting bitten. They put themselves first. They also would shelter us from the rain. They were the ones that would get wet and cover us up, or on cold nights put a blanket on us. Shelter means a place giving temporary protection from bad weather or danger.

You may have never been protected the way that you needed. You may be the child that was harmed coming up by parents, family, friends, and even your job. I want you to release it. Get into the arms who wants to protect you from danger seen and unseen. The Lord is the best example of shelter. He loves protecting His children. He knows what's ahead and what's behind us. We just have to fully Trust the LORD to protect us. You may be wonder how do I fully let God shelter me? We start by giving Him our heart. Then We take steps daily to draw closer to the LORD. Like we would do being in a relationship.

Psalms 91 Whoever lives under the shelter of the Highest will remain in the shadow of the Almighty. ² I will say to the LORD, "⌐ You are ⌐ my refuge and my fortress, my God in whom I trust." ³ He is the one who will rescue you from hunters' traps and from deadly plagues. ⁴ He will cover you with his feathers, and under his wings you will find refuge. His truth is your shield and armor. ⁵ You do not need to fear terrors of the night, arrows that fly during the day.

When we think about shelter we think about protection, a roof over our heads, guidance through a situation. We all need guidance through life. God will lead and guide us in the right direction. We just have to know His voice.

Prayer

Father God we just say thank you for being our shelter in the time of a storm. Help us to stay under your wing. Lord if we are under the wrong place help us remove ourselves from toxic people and places. Lord God thank you for drawing us closer to you. Lord thank you for the word to help ud to see that hiding in you id the best shelter from the outside. We give you praise that we are still here in Jesus name Amen.

Day 11

Study

Time to dive in deeper

Are you ready to study the word?

Growing in the word can change your life for good. Many of us never like studying homework. Some felt to good or even felt like it was to hard. I've learned that it is very important to study. Here's why

Stay in the word Staying in the word helps you to know Him. It keeps you secure.

> **John 15: 7-9 If you abide in Me, and My words abide in you, you will ask what you desire, and it shall be done for you. By this My Father is glorified, that you bear much fruit; so you will be My disciples. "As the Father loved Me, I also have loved you; abide in My love.**

Teach it to self and others. You can't teach what you don't know. You must learn it.

> **2 Timothy 2:2 You have heard me teach things that have been confirmed by many reliable witnesses. Now teach these truths to other trustworthy people who will be able to pass them on to others.**

Understand what we are reading.

> **Psalms 119:105 "Your word is a lamp to guide my feet and a light for my path."**

Be **D**elivered from our sins

Psalms 51:14 New International Version (NIV) Deliver me from the guilt of bloodshed, O God, you who are God my Savior, and my tongue will sing of your righteousness.

Yearn for more of God

> **Psalms 119:166 -170 NIV 166 I wait for your salvation, LORD, AND I follow your commands.   167 I obey your statutes, for I love them greatly. 168 I obey your precepts and your statutes, for all my ways are known to you. 169 May my cry come before you, LORD give me understanding according to your word. 170 May my supplication come before you; deliver me according to your promise.**

Prayer

Simply stop and say thank you for showing me how to dive deeper in your word. Love you more than anything. I'm learning to **S**tay in you so that I can **T**each others how to walk in you. Thank you for giving me the knowledge to **U**nderstand situations when they show up in my life. Thank you for **D**elivering me from my past trauma and all my shame. **Y**earning for you daily because it your presence that I want. Thank you in Jesus name Amen.

Day 12

SURE

NO **YES**

Are you SURE your mind is made up?

Having some doubt… What is having you to make unsure decisions? Being unsure can lead you down the wrong path or take you off track of your destination. People say all the time when you study long you study wrong. It can be very challenging to make wise decisions. Every day we wake up we have to make a decision if we want to do good or bad. It is in your mind. We must stop wasting time making poor decisions. Growing up as a little girl I let others make up my mind for me. I was afraid to give an answer for myself. It's time to make a stand and believe in making wise decisions.

One of the best keys to life is being sure of what you want. When you go to a restaurant you tend to look over things until you are sure of what you want. Even in groceries stores. It may be hard to make good decisions, but it helps us to know that we all have a mind of our own. Even as a baby they will let you know when they are hungry or needed to be change, maybe even if they felt uncomfortable.

The question is how do you become **SURE** about it? You must BE…

1. **S**atisfied with your answer.
2. **U**nwavering not worried about anything Standing firm in what we believe.
3. **R**eal about what you decided on.
4. **E**nduring all the way to the end

Philippians 1:6 And I am sure of this, that he who began a good work in you will bring it to completion at the day of Jesus Christ.

1 Thessalonians 5:23 Now may the God of peace himself sanctify you completely, and may your whole spirit and soul and body be kept blameless at the coming of our Lord Jesus Christ. 24 He who calls you is faithful; he will surely do it.

Prayer

God we just say thank you for keeping your promises. We thank you for being **Satisfied** with sending your son to die on the cross for our sins. **Unwavering** a God who never changes. You are simply amazing in everything that you do. God we thank you for being **REAL.** Nothing about you is a lie. You are trustworthy God. Lord thank you for **ENDURING** through the storms with us. There is no one that can compare to you. LORD help us to be SURE in who you are, that when we say YES we say it with our heart and not just because someone told us. Deliver us from wrong thinking in JESUS name AMEN!

Day 13

INJECTION TIME

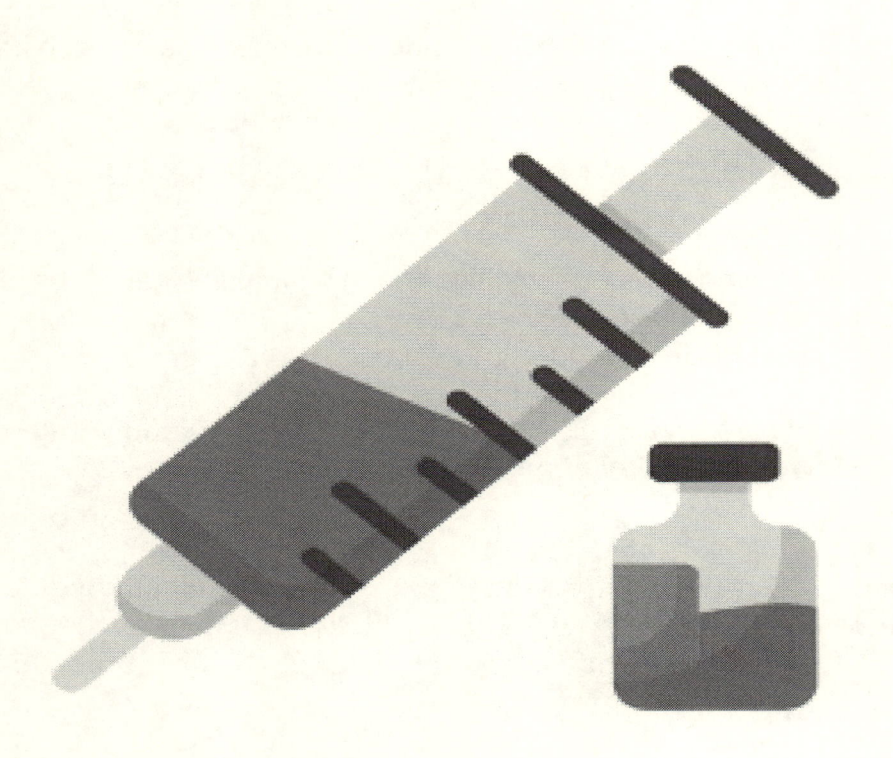

Are you getting the right meds?

What have you injected in you that has mess you up on the inside. We tend to take meds to help with pain to feel a void. When we were sick, we need medicine to get well. As babies giving them medicine was like trying to give them dirt. One thing medicine does is make us all better. We find strength in getting well. People tend to say meds can cure a loth or issues. The question is... What happens to us when inject the wrong meds into our system? We began to have setbacks. Some of die from the wrong injection. Are you tired of injecting the wrong medicine in your body? I know I was. I knew I had to get the right doctor to fix my situation.

Look at it on the spiritual side of this. God sent us all the best prescription, his son JESUS. Or should I say doctor Jesus. He's the right formula to handle all of our needs. When you are down and can't seem to bounce back Jesus sends us Joy, Peace and so much Love. We have to be open to giving God our heart so he can work on us. Trust me it was the best decision that I have made in my life. To be healed, and made whole is something I strive for daily. I ask the LORD to inject me with the right medicine so that I know how to go out and handle God's children. We can't inject others with a filthy heart.

**Psalm 103:2-6 NIV ² Praise the LORD, my soul, and forget not all his benefits—
³ who forgives all your sins and heals all your diseases, ⁴ who redeems your life from the pit and crowns you with love and compassion, ⁵ who satisfies your desires with good things so that your youth is renewed like the eagle's.
⁶ The LORD works righteousness and justice for all the oppressed.**

Prayer

Dear LORD we want to stop and say thank you for injecting us with your powerful word. Thank you for not giving up on us. Thank you for being there for us when we are sick and almost at death bed. You step in and help us get right. Thank you for helping us see that we need your meds daily. Show us how to come to you and get free from our dirty flesh. Thank you LORD for helping us make it out the hospital and back into the world. We stand bold in knowing you're the best doctor, in JESUS name AMEN!

DAY 14

Intimacy with the LORD

Experiencing the depth of love through bonding...

Father & Me... Everyone has someone in their life that you have a strong foundation with that no one can break. It took trusting that person with your whole life. Something that didn't happen overnight, baby steps right... When we look at Intimacy what do you see? We see closeness, a private cozy atmosphere. Your relationship be so close that some people want let a stumbling block knock them down. It's a ride or die type of relationship. What happens when that close bond with someone change or fall? Most of us tend to try to build new ones with people just to feel a void because the last one never worked out.

One of the best decisions that I have ever made was building a relationship with the LORD? It was like me being a baby again. He listened to me without cutting me off, He felt my pain, understood my tears, calmed my worry, and also eased my past. He the best friend I have ever had. He changed my life. It was like me being that seed that need water to grow. No one can separate me from the LOVE of God. Our bound so tight now that I go to him when I need help making transitions.

After all, what would you think of someone who claimed to be your friend, but was consistently unfaithful and disloyal to you? Would you consider that person a "REAL" friend? Probably not we would cut them off. Our friendship with God is thus practically demonstrated through our loyalty, allegiance and obedience to Him

John 15:14 You are my friends if you do what I command. 15 I no longer call you servants, because a servant does not know his master's business. Instead, I have called you friends, for everything that I learned from my Father I have made known to you.

Psalm 63:1: "O God, you are my God; earnestly I seek you; my soul thirsts for you; my flesh faints for you, as in a dry and weary land where there is no water."

Prayer

God, we stop and say thank you for being the best example of friendship. You love us past all of our mistakes. God we just say thank you for not turning your back on us. Lord if we struggle with being a loyal friend to someone else, please help us. Forgive us for lying on others. Thank you for shaping us into better sons and daughters. Friends look out for one another, stick up for one another, and remain true to one another. Thank you for being that and more in Jesus' name Amen.

Day 15

Increase your belief!

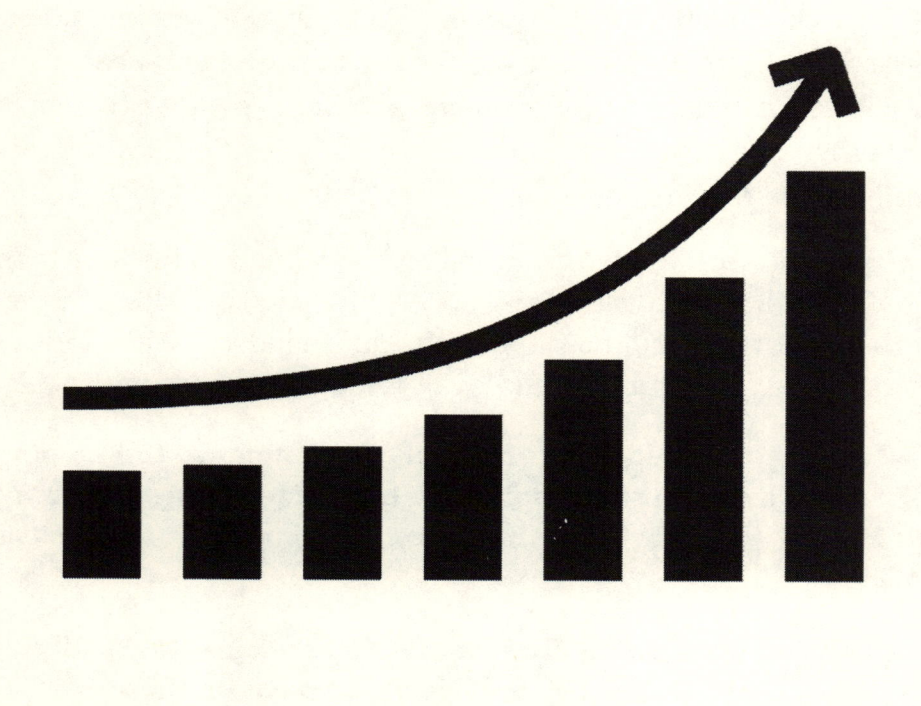

New Levels

Are you ready for more? Everyone loves hearing the word increase. Especially when it comes to finances. When our boss gives us a promotion, we know it comes with a higher pay. Or what about us as children when our parents use to say I'm going to increase your allowance. Maybe it never happened to you like that but at some point, in your life you have increase in something. Look at your life now, as you see you are not that same person you were 3 or maybe even ten years ago. Stop and give yourself a hand. You have become stronger now than before.

The question was asked, are you ready for more? I know you may be thinking yes, I need more money because I'm still having a hard time meeting the needs of all my bills. Well, this may hurt your feelings, but we all need to increase in the LORD. He wants to give you more but you are stuck in the in the same door that the Lord is trying to push you out of. Increasing in Him will open up so many blessings that you never would imagine. They say favor isn't fair, but it is to those who put in the work. Have you ever been so hungry that when you started eating you felt your strength coming back. Well, that's how it is in God. If you put your time in with Him the increase will come in your walk, talk, the way you live. Its time to grow and increase in God.

Luke 17:5-6 5 The apostles said to the Lord, "Increase our faith!" 6 He replied, "If you have faith as small as a mustard seed, you can say to this mulberry tree, 'Be uprooted and planted in the sea,' and it will obey you.

2 Peter 3:17-18 17 Therefore, dear friends, since you have been forewarned, be on your guard so that you may not be carried away by the error of the lawless and fall from your secure position. 18 But grow in the grace and knowledge of our Lord and Savior Jesus Christ. To him be glory both now and forever! Amen.

Prayer

Lord, thank you for the increase that you've already done. We pray that you continue to show us how to decrease so that you can increase in our life and in our heart. Forgive us for not praying more, and studying more. Lord, we mark today that we seek you in everything that we do. Thank you for protecting us we love you and desire you more. If we don't know how Lord show us how, in Jesus' name Amen.

Day 16

Believe in yourself!

SORRY Get up and go stand in the mirror, look at yourself and say I'm sorry. Sorry for counting yourself out, beating yourself up, not encouraging yourself. You are about to take back your life and begin to face you. We should not keep harming ourselves with what others have called us. You can make it out, you will make it out. I used to let others speak their affirmations over my life. It caused me to be put in a dark place with who I was. I never knew Whitley until I ask God to show me who I was. I begin weeping. God said get up and look at yourself. He shown me the beauty that was on the inside hiding because I was too afraid to embrace me. I'm not that person anymore. I have apologized for making mistakes, lying, and misleading Whitley. If I can do it, I know you can too. We have to also say sorry for how we have mistreated people. We all are God's children. Sorry means feeling distress, especially through sympathy with someone else's misfortune.

The Lord desires for us to heal from the pain of hurting one another. When you apologize, do so sincerely, as the Lord looks at the heart and knows our true intentions. We have all caused hurt, and after forgiving ourselves, what is the next step? We must seek God to heal us completely and embrace new beginnings.

Psalm 38:18 ESV / 41 I confess my iniquity; I am sorry for my sin.

Psalm 51:10-12 Create in me a pure heart, O God, and renew a steadfast spirit within me. Do not cast me from your presence or take your Holy Spirit from me. Restore to me the joy of your salvation and grant me a willing spirit, to sustain me.

Matthew 5:9 ESV / 37
"Blessed are the peacemakers, for they shall be called sons of God.

Prayer

Lord, thank you for teaching us how to forgive ourselves. Thank you for showing us that it's alright to see ourselves the way that you see us. Lord, you are love, peace and joy. Continue to help us heal from the things that has hurt us. Lord and sorry for not seeing you as the father that you are. Thank you for allowing us to confess what's in our hearts in JESUS name, AMEN.

Day 17

SUPPLY

He understands the needs of every one of us and provides the necessary supplies.

He Supplies all of our needs... What Supplies do you have? We love shopping for supplies, whether it's online or in person. Everyone needs many different supplies when preparing for work. Many people love shopping for things that they need. Seems to feel like a fresh slate. Growing up my mom always made sure we had the right supplies, whether it was school, a job, church. My Mama taught me how to manage supplies. Making a list really help me organize my agenda. What happens when you are unprepared for the assignment. We tend to get throwed off with a schedule. Life seemed to be shattered. Have you ever just stopped and realized that this life we live in is all about supplies. Some things that are on the supply list we don't need but we keep anyways. What type of supplies are you carrying that you need to get rid of... Have a moment to really think about it. You may just have the wrong thing in your life that is misleading you. When signing a check you don't use a pencil to sign because it can be erased. You sign with ink. So having the right supplies daily can help you through life.

The LORD is the best supplier we need. When we are struggling Lord steps in and save the day. He knows what we need and when we need it. He owns everything. The LORD guides us with the right tools like knowing how to love our enemies, bless those who are in need, even encourage others along the way. What ever you may be struggling in the LORD will send you the right supplies. If you don't know Trust HIM. He will never let you down.

Philippians 4:6 NIV Do not be anxious about anything, but in every situation, by prayer and petition, with thanksgiving, present your requests to God

Philippians 4:19 NIV And my God will meet all your needs according to the riches of his glory in Christ Jesus.

Psalms 23[1] The LORD is my shepherd, I lack nothing. [2] He makes me lie down in green pastures, He leads me beside quiet waters, [3] He refreshes my soul. He guides me along the right paths for his name's sake.[4] Even though I walk through the darkest valley,[a] I will fear no evil, for you are with me; your rod and your staff, they comfort me. [5] You prepare a table before me in the presence of my enemies. You anoint my head with oil; my cup overflows. [6] Surely your goodness and love will follow me all the days of my life, and I will dwell in the house of the LORD forever.

Prayer

Lord God, I want to stop and say Thank you for being my supplier. Thank you for guiding me let something's go that I don't need. I lack nothing in you LORD. Help me to see the right supplies. Fix me LORD, my heart my mind. You see all, you know all things. LORD continue to put me in the right position with the right supplies. I trust your plans in JESUS name, AMEN!!!

Day 18

TRANSFORMATION

Clean me up LORD!

God can transform your life… Ever wanted a transformation. Have you ever woken up and look in the mirror and didn't like what you saw. Often people try to change the outer appearance. I didn't use to love myself. I let others create who they thought I should be. Suffering with insecurities will have you submitting to the wrong people. Transformation was a struggle in my past, that I had to seek God to help me. I didn't know how to transform into who the Lord was calling me. It took prayer, fasting and staying in His word.

God Knows how to take your flaws, your scars and bruises and clean you up and give you a clean slate. The LORD don't want us stuck in that situation for the rest of our life. He wants to change your attire, from the inside and outside. Being transformed in the LORD is like taking a bath. He is not going to miss any spots. He's so perfect. Ask yourself are you ready to be transformed in the LORD.

Romans 12:2 (NIV) Do not conform to the pattern of this world, but be transformed by the renewing of your mind. Then you will be able to test and approve what God's will is his good, pleasing and perfect will.

2 Corinthians 5:17 (NIV) Therefore, if anyone is in Christ, the new creation has come:[a] The old has gone, the new is here!

Prayer
Lord, thank you for my transformation. Help me to continue to transform into a better me. Help me to take off what needs to be taken off and put on the fullness of you. Lord, when I don't see my layers of dead skin help to reveal it. Thank you for looking past my flaws and reaching my heart in Jesus name Amen.

Day 19

Test

(Here comes the storm)

Ready or not, the storm is coming.

Are you prepared for a storm? Have you prepared for the Test yet. When the teacher hands out a paper and say study this you will be tested on it Friday. We begin to go home and study to make sure we are ready to past the test. Some think they know so well that they say they have it and don't need to Study because they are smart. What if the teacher gives you a test that is so tricky that you know you are not prepared for. What happens when life throws you a curve ball? What happens when you see a bad storm is coming and you are not prepared with the proper things you need to whether it? I have had many test in my life that if I didn't lean on God it would have taken me out. I wasn't always strong. When the doctor told me they saw a spot on my baby lung. I was afraid. I didn't know what to do. I had to pray through it. I must say Prayer is a powerful weapon when you know who you are praying too. The storm Got so big that I wanted to just cry every day. The Lord said where is your faith. I knew then that I had to seek him more. God sure turned it around.

You feel the wind and see the dark clouds. It's about to storm. Here comes the test. You can still make it out alright because the LORD is in the midst of it all. Although it seems to be pouring down with lighting and thunder. The Lord is teaching you how to stand in it and not be moved by things in the world. Your friends may have left you but He's still there. You may have gotten bad news from the doctor, but the LORD knows how to be a doctor in a sick room, even fight a tough court case. He's a great lawyer. Whatever you need Him to be that He is. He's so amazing. Nobody can compare to you. Everyone handles storms different. Know the difference from a test from God and when it's from Satan. Adam & Eve was in the garden and God told them what to not do. They had ever good thing they ever wanted. God gave them that. They had one test and that was to not eat from a certain tree in the garden. Eve was talked into disobeying God. **(Gensis 3)** Be careful who you allow to trick you into felling the test. If the Lord gives you an assignment obey it the first time. Trust me, you have to use discernment and know if it's from God or Satan. Some storms can cause you to die in them. I've learned to listen to the voice of God. To past any test it comes with prayer, fasting, consecration, meditating….

Colossians 3:23 Whatever you do, work at it with all your heart, as working for the Lord, not for human masters.

James 1:2-4 Count it all joy, my brothers, when you meet trials of various kinds, for you know that the testing of your faith produces steadfastness. And let steadfastness have its full effect, that you may be perfect and complete, lacking in nothing

Proverbs 3:26 For the LORD will be your confidence and will keep your foot from being caught.

Prayer
Lord, forgive me for listening to myself and not you. Lord thank you for helping me past the test. When I am tempted to do wrong thank you for helping me past the Test. Thank you for showing me my issues. Lord you are so good. You didn't create test for us to fail but you did to get the Glory. Thank you that from this day forward that I will trust your voice in Jesus name Amen.

Day 20

Testify

You've achieved it—now declare it!

It's TIME..... Others need to hear your story, of how God delivered you? Are you ready to testify about how good the Lord has been to you. You made it through the transformation, and the Test. So what's standing in your way. Some didn't make it to give there testimony. I want you to stop and just give the Lord Praise for making it to Day 20. Testify, I know there was some hard days, crying night, and you may have wanted to give up on a few. Look at what the Lord has brought you through. I know it wasn't easy and its alright to shed some tears but Testify about how loving and patience that the Lord has been with you.

Aren't you glad to see the sunshine after a long storm. Take a deep breath because without the Lord we are nothing. We got freed from guilt, shame, hurt, abuse, lies, anger, our dirty ways. You don't suffer from depression, loneliness, abuse, so many things. I want you to go through today and Testify to someone how the Lord has change your life. Watch how it will make you feel to know what was once your struggle is now your Testimony story.

2 Timothy 1:8 "Therefore, never be ashamed of the testimony about our Lord or of me, his prisoner. Instead, by God's power, join me in suffering for the sake of the gospel.

Matthew 10:32 "Everyone who acknowledges me publicly here on earth, I will also acknowledge before my Father in heaven.

Prayer

Hallelujah, to the Amazing Father you are. Lord I praise you for all you've done for me. Thank you for allowing me to make it outto tell my story. Thank you for guiding me with your hands. Lord I love you, adore you give you honor and glory for the rest of my life. In Jesus name, Amen

Day 21

Effort

GIVE IT YOUR ALL!

Are you giving it your all? Have you put forward the effort in the Lord? The more you climb the harder it will become. You have to keep going no matter what, even when you want to give up. I was once at the stage of giving up because I didn't want to give effort. They say you can't get out something you don't put in. Effort means conscious exertion of power: hard work. a job requiring time and effort: a serious attempt: try. making an effort to reduce costs. After working hard and putting in the effort you will soon benefit from the award. Being on a team in order to win you have to put in an effort. God put forth the best effort when He sent His only Son to die for us all.

The Lord taught me so many things about effort. I knew you had to put in the work but you had to actually give it your all. So many of us try to fake our way to the top. When you do that it shows up in your work. Don't be lazy with it. Don't even lie in it. The Lord will open up so many doors if we put in the effort. In order to see change you have to keep fighting through.

2 Peter 1:5 Now for this very reason also, applying all diligence, in your faith supply moral excellence, and in your moral excellence, knowledge,

Ecclesiastes 5:3 For the dream comes through much effort and the voice of a fool through many words.

Prayer

Lord we simply thank you for being the best example for effort. You never set down on us. You always showed up on time. Lord continue to guide us in putting forth the effort. When we feel like we want to slack give us the strength to keep going, to keep trusting, to keep walking and believing. In Jesus name Amen.

Day 22

Elevation

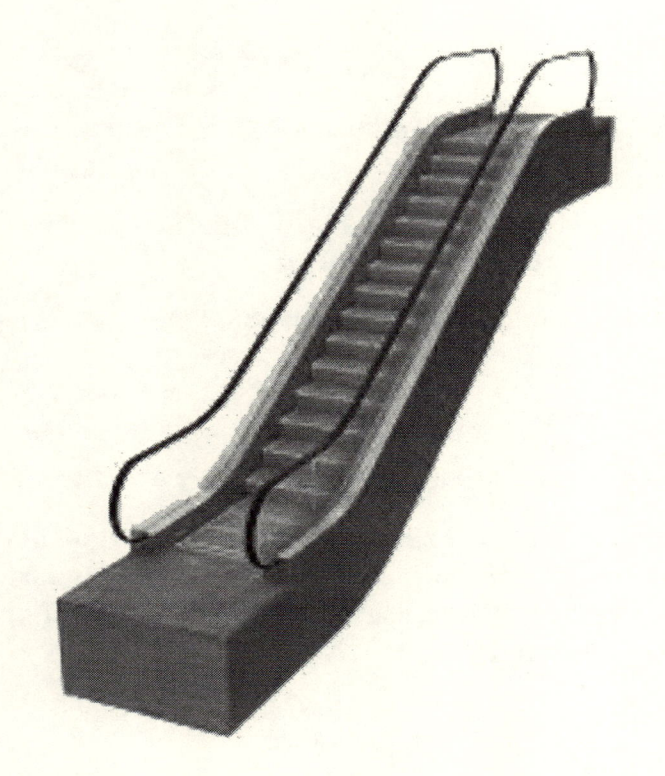

(God is calling you higher)

Have you ever wanted to go higher? In life most of us strive to reach another level. Whether it's in school, job or just in our career path. Have you ever walked in a room and realize that there was something missing. Or there was more in you that you had to offer but was afarid to let it out. If you are in a place where you are stuck and don't know how to make it out. Tell yourself "Its Elevation Time." You can't stay down in the desert. God is calling you higher. Elevation means the action or fact of elevating or being elevated, or height above a given level, especially sea level. When God elevates you no one can take that from you. Our jobs, may fire or demote us but God has the final say so. Many may be jealous, or simply don't understand that you have been elevated.

Growing up I have always wondered how do you make it to the top. People have seen to be the driver in my life. When others are driving for you, they can sometimes have you to miss turns, or even the destination that God was placing you at. I had to get out of the passenger seat and into the driving seat. I had to find out God for myself, and let Him lead and guide me to the right place. God told me He didn't want me on formula. It was time for some heavy meat. It's time you allow God in completely and take over your life. Allow Him to speak to you and put you in places that no one else can do.

James 4:10 Humble yourselves before the LORD, and He will lift you up.

Matthew 6:33 KJV But seek ye first the kingdom of God, and his righteousness; and all these things shall be added unto you.

This is a word that God was giving to me for someone who is reading this and is wondering... God is getting ready to promote you to another level in Him. Be Prepared, Be Praying, Be Patient. It's going to happen when you least expect it.

Prayer

Father God, we thank you for the door of opportunities. We thank you for moving us in rooms and in front of others that sees what you see in us. God you are simply Amazing. Thank you for freeing us from our past. God we thank you that in due time you will elevate us. Teach us how to stay Humble in Jesus, name Amen.

Day 23

Early AM....

It's praying time...

How early will you make time for the Lord? Making time is the best things anyone of us can do. For the one who has all power in His hand. Are you struggling in that area. You can be on the edge of a breakthrough and all you need is that alone time with the LORD. Worship and pray your way to Him. Its in the early morning hours where the Lord wants to talk to you and show us how much you mean to Him.

Have you ever woken up and look at the clock and saw that it's 3 a.m…. Many of us turn over and go back to sleep. When it presents itself to you again, wake up. I know its early, but the Lord wants to speak to you. God wakes me up like this many times. Have you ever thought about why. It be a divine appointments. It's the best time when ever one else in the house may be sleep. Its peaceful. I begin to worship my way to Him. In was in my worship and praying where God begin to show me things. Or sometime to pray for others. We never know what's to come, that's why the Lord have us up early. I hear people say, Early birds catch deals. When going shopping you begin to catch all kinds of things.

Proverbs 8:17 I love those who love me, And those who seek me diligently will find me.

Psalms 63:1-3 O God, thou art my God; early will I seek thee: my soul thirsteth for thee, my flesh longeth for thee in a dry and thirsty land, where no water is; ² To see thy power and thy glory, so as I have seen thee in the sanctuary. ³ Because thy lovingkindness is better than life, my lips shall praise thee.

Prayer

Lord, we simply say thank you for opening our eyes to dwell in you. Lord you rise us up early to soak in you. Help us to see what we need to see. Help us to understand what we need to do. Father, we simply thank you for being everything that we need you to be. Lord, we pray that we can continue to obey your voice. We pray that we will lean into you. Forgive us for not submitting to your plans. We love you and adore you in Jesus name Amen.

Day 24

New

You never know what God has in Store for you…

Ever got tired of the old and wanted something new. Whether if it was the way your life has always been. Most of us get tired of looking at the same thing year after year. Its time for something new. We desire so much such as new cars, houses, clothes, shoes, jobs. The list can go on and on but how do our outer appearance look in God's eye? We dress up for the world but on the inside, we are still carrying the old things. The Lord wants us to get rid of it so that He can bless us with new. Stop and really examine your heart.

Not only do we get tired of the way we live. Some of us get tired of what we drive, or our attire, or maybe even the company we keep. Wrong company attracts mess. The Lord knows the best plan for our life. We must continue to seek His will. When the Lord blesses us with new things no one can take that away. Some of us may feel like we not good enough we have to learn to live the negativity at the door and not let it in. So lets learn to make room for new things in the LORD. His word says be not afraid.

Isaiah 43:19
"For I am about to do something new. See, I have already begun! Do you not see it? I will make a pathway through the wilderness. I will create rivers in the dry wasteland."

Deuteronomy 31:8 "Do not be afraid or discouraged, for the Lord will personally go ahead of you. He will be with you; he will neither fail you nor abandon you."

Psalms 32:8 "The Lord says, "I will guide you along the best pathway for your life. I will advise you and watch over you.

Proverbs 3:5-6 "Seek his will in all you do, and he will show you which path to take. Trust in the Lord with all your heart; do not depend on your own understanding."

Prayer

Lord we simply say thank you for opening up our hearts and our minds to see the things that are in you. Continue to help us break off from our old ways so that we can truly embrace you. Help us discern the company that we keep. You are perfect in all your ways. We thank you for the NEW that is already taken place in our life, and in our hearts. Let the scriptures set in our heart to trust your words. You will never leave us nor forsake us, in Jesus name. Amen.

The Lord is about to lead you through another door that no man can shut. Trust the process. The LORD wants you to walk into it amazed. New things no one will be able to stop it. I speak NEWNESS in your career, homes, health, and in your heart.

Day 25

Nourishing (Fruits)

Do you have good or rotten Fruit?

Are you ready to be nourished in the LORD. Take time out today to open up and allow Him to nourish you so that the growth can start. You must take the course for something healthy. Don't look at like its to much. As a baby is born in the world someone has to nurture it. A baby needs to be fed to help it develop and grow. Nourish means to develop, to nurture, to lift up. Ask yourself, who is Nourishing you?

Its time that we allow God to nurture us in to the person He wants us to be. That comes with, reading the word, fasting, and praying. When your soul is nourished, you will flourish. You are the seed that God has planted. He wants to nourish us in His word. We will soon develop the fruits of Him love, joy, peace, forbearance, kindness, goodness, faithfulness, gentleness and self-control.

Get the Dirt and a seed
1. **Plant the seed** (That putting your faith in God)
2. **Water it** (Read the word soak it up. Mediate on it)
3. **Watch it Grow** (Praying & and fasting)

<u>Galatians 5:22-23</u> 22 But the fruit of the Spirit is love, joy, peace, forbearance, kindness, goodness, faithfulness, 23 gentleness and self-control. Against such things there is no law.

<u>John 6:35</u> And Jesus said unto them, I am the bread of life: he that cometh to me shall never hunger; and he that believeth on me shall never thirst.

<u>1 Peter 2:2</u>
Like newborn infants, long for the pure spiritual milk, that by it you may grow up into salvation

<u>Matthew 4:4</u>
But he answered, "It is written, "'Man shall not live by bread alone, but by every word that comes from the mouth of God.

Prayer

Lord we come to you saying thank you for the nourishments that you have poured in us. Lord help us to continue to soak in you. Help us to carry the fruits of you so we can walk in tell others of the goodness of you. Lord we desire to taste more of you daily, not with our mouth but also in our hearts. Show us how to feed your people in Jesus name, Amen

Day 26

Challenge

Are you prepared to go to WAR?

Conquer the Challenges

Challenges can be hard, but it's worth the race. Many of us love to challenges others at things. We say things like, "We got this," or "This is easy." What happens when the Lord puts us up for the challenge? Situations that we haven't faced. Some of us can admit we gave up. Well the Lord doesn't give us challenges that will harm us. He gives us challenges to overcome our battles. He teaches us how to live right. Its not easy but its worth it. With Faith we can do all things.

Philippians 4:13 I can do all things through Christ that strengthen me.

I hated challenges that I knew I couldn't win at least that what I thought. When you walk in challenges with doubt it begin to cause you to fail at things. When David went up against Goliath he went up in faith. David knew it was a challenge. He had confident that the God wouldn't let him fall. His faith was so strong that doubt never crossed his mind. Even when others told him He couldn't do it. He passed it because of God on his side.

I challenged you to put your faith in the LORD! He knows what's best for us. Every assignment that the LORD has told you walk through it in faith. No matter if it on your job, at church, around family trust God through the process. Allow Him to lead you.

Psalm 46:1: "God is our refuge and strength, an ever-present help in trouble."

Deuteronomy 31:6: "Be strong and courageous. Do not be afraid or terrified because of them, for the LORD your God goes with you; he will never leave you nor forsake you."

Peter 4:12: Beloved, think it not strange concerning the fiery trial which is to try you, as though some strange thing happened unto you.

Prayer

God, we thank you for the challenges that you have allowed us to grow through. We thank you for the strength to come for the journey. Help us to see that we can go through anything with the strength of you. When we are down continue to lift us up. You are all powerful, and all knowing. Thank you for helping us conquering our fears. We love you and praise you in Jesus name, Amen.

Day 27

Company

Share with the LORD,

who and what is keeping you company.

Who is at your house that may be keeping you from hearing the Lord? All companies are not good company. You may have some people in your life right now who you need to pull away from. Lean in to hear the voice of the LORD and ask for discernment who will needs to be removed. There're people who are setting plots, speaking curses, and some just want to know your business. They are not your friends; they are more like a frienemy. A "frienemy" is a blend of "friend" and "enemy." This term is used to describe someone who appears to be a friend but actually behaves in a harmful or competitive way.

Learning about the company shifted my life. I got tired of hanging around people that couldn't pray for me. They want to see me do good. No one like to feel unwanted so why attach yourself to people who can encourage you as you encourage them. You don't need someone Preying over your life. On this season of your life you must let the negative go and attach yourself to good company. Company that will motivate, pray, fast, and really hear from the LORD. Good **COMPANY** will always keep you on the right track. It's the bad company that corrupts evil traits. We must keep our eyes and mind on the LORD. Be mindful of who you attach to in the season of your life. The Lord wants to put us with the right people but we must let go of the bad ones and get around positive ones that will **C**over you in prayer. Help **O**bserve the ones that are not for you. Always **M**otivate, **P**our, and **A**ppreciate, a **N**ever-ending **Y**ou.

Psalms 1:1 **Blessed is the one who does not walk in step with the wicked or stand in the way that sinners take or sit in the company of mockers.**

1 Corinthians 15:33 **Do not be misled: "Bad company corrupts good character."**

2 Corinthians 6:14 **Do not be yoked together with unbelievers. For what do righteousness and wickedness have in common? Or what fellowship can light have with darkness?**

1 John 4:1 **Dear friends, do not believe every spirit, but test the spirits to see whether they are from God, because many false prophets have gone out into the world.**

Prayer

Lord we simply thank you for being the best example of company. You have never failed us as a Father, Teacher, Mentor. We say thank you for showing us the right company to keep. Lord change our hearts. If we are in the bad company deliver us from lying, gossiping tongues. Show us how to live how you want us to live. Forgives us for not being a leader. Teach us how to use our words to love and not tare down you people, in Jesus name, AMEN.

Day 28

Cover

Wouldn't you prefer the right kind of protection?

Who's covering you?

Being in a cold room will have you finding blankets to cover up. I know I don't like to be cold, but I love being covered up. Cover keeps us warm, and comfortable. Growing up our parents was our cover. They protected us from many things and people. It's like bringing a newborn baby home. The first thing we do is take a blanket and cover our little ones. If they couldn't cover us they gave us to someone who could. You might feel like you never was covered the right way. No matter if it was raining our parents still covered us. If it was after a bath, they had a towel to wrap us in, or maybe it was raining. They covered us with a coat, or umbrella. No matter what it was they made sure we was safe, and warm.

Maybe you have been searching for the right covering. Just like you have to watch your company you also have to watch who is covering you. The best covering is the LORD. He covers us from so much. We just have to trust in Him and allow Him to be our covering. Think back over your life that car crash or the bullet that could have taken you out. Cancer that you didn't see how you made it out cancer free. The Lord has been covering you and still been covering you. Stop and give the LORD praise. He goes before us. He covers the whole word. I truly thank the LORD for covering me. He block many things in our life. Allow Him to be the pilot in your life. He's the Towel when we are wet, that cover when we are cold. He's also the eye when we are blind.

Psalms 91:2-4) 2 I will say of the Lord, "He is my refuge and my fortress, my God, in whom I trust." 3 Surely he will save you from the fowler's snare and from the deadly pestilence. 4 He will cover you with his feathers, and under his wings you will find refuge; his faithfulness will be your shield and rampart.

John 10: 28-30 28 I give them eternal life, and they shall never perish; no one will snatch them out of my hand. 29 My Father, who has given them to me, is greater than all; no one can snatch them out of my Father's hand. 30 I and the father are one."

Prayer

Lord, I stop to say thank you for covering me and showing me you. Thank you that you didn't let me die in my sins. Continue to lead me. Thank you for protecting me. Lord you are everything I need you to be. If I am under the wrong covering deliver me from it. Show me how to stay in the right covering. Heal my heart from my past issues. This day forward I trust you in Jesus, name AMEN.

Day 29

Are you Yielding when you see the sign?

What are you yielding to? Are you yielding to the Holy Spirit. He's trying to guide you on the right path. You may be like that car that drives slowly to the yielding sign. Don't hesitate in the season that you are in. Allow God lead you where you need to go. Stop allowing others to lead you. When yielding you have to be cautious. Yield means to produce or provide (a natural, agricultural, or industrial product) give way to arguments, demands, or pressure. Just as a yield sign indicates you should let someone else go ahead of you, yielding to LORD means we surrender our lives and commit to follow Him and let Him lead. Surrendering to the Lord is the best commitment anyone of us can do. Are you willing to give up your old ways to follow Christ? He's the one that can add or subtract from our lives. I hear the LORD say Yield to me my child. All the heavy things you have been carrying give it to the LORD.

I've gotten through some of the rough season because I yield to the LORD. It wasn't easy. If you find yourself at a stand still not knowing which way to go we must stand still and yield in to the LORD's voice.

Psalm 37:4 Take delight in the LORD **and he will give you the desires of your heart.**

James 3:17 But the wisdom that comes from heaven is first of all pure; then peace-loving, considerate, submissive, full of mercy and good fruit, impartial and sincere.

James 4:7 Submit yourselves, then, to God. Resist the devil, and he will flee from you.

Prayer

Lord, we just want to slow down and yield to you. Lord, teach us how to submit to your will and your ways. Help us to yield to your word. If there is anything that is hindering us to seek you remove it in Jesus name. Lord, show us how to pray more. We say thank you for being the in front of us to show us the way. Lord, we love you and thank you in Jesus name, Amen

Days 30

Years

Years are like chapters in the book of life; each one brings its own story, filled with moments of joy, lessons learned, and growth that shapes who we become.

Looking back over your life how God has graced you down through the years. He's been so amazing to us. We all can say we came along way. His grace and mercy have carried us through some tough trials and tribulations. We can truly say we kept the faith in knowing that He can still do it and will do it. If you are wondering when, just know timing is all in God's hand. He can add years to all our life.

I struggle with Pain, Heartache, Trauma in so many years of my life. I wanted to throw in the towel. The Lord reminded me of the woman with the issue of blood. She suffered for 12 years. I was crying over one year. I repented immediately. The Lord was showing me that in the years of suffering He still can heal, and break us free from bondage. Pain don't last long in God's eye. Find what you have been dealing with down through the years, and surrender it to God so He can do it in the right timing.

Joel 2:25-26 (ESV) I will restore to you the years that the swarming locust has eaten, the hopper, the destroyer, and the cutter, my great army, which I sent among you. "You shall eat in plenty and be satisfied, and praise the name of the LORD your God, who has dealt wondrously with you.

Prayer

Lord, we want to simply say thank you for the years we have made it too so far. We ask that you help us heal from the suffering that we have endured through the years. We want a fresh and renewed mind in you. Lord, we take this time to mediate on your words. You have always been faithful and true. We give you glory in Jesus name, Amen.

Day 31

YOU DID IT!!!

YOU ROCK!!!

CELEBRATE YOURSELF

YOU'VE COMPLETED 31 DAYS OF CONSISTENCY WITH THE LORD!

You have made it to 31 days of being CONSISTENT with the LORD. Give your self a hand. God is well pleased with your progress. Take today and Pray and begin to reflect over the things you have learned and study. Its so much to take in but its worth the GROWTH. I am proud of the progress. I know it wasn't easy, You may had to start over a few days. It's okay. Growing in the LORD is a daily walk. So, I admire all the hard word you had to put in to get to this day. If nobody told you just know God is pleased and so am I. You can continue your days in growing in HIM. We all trying to just make it to Heaven. You took the first step to **Choose** the Lord so that He can help you **Change** for him and now you are **Committed** to Him. Just keep **Obeying** the LORD and watch Him **Open** up doors for you. You will know it because of the **OIL** that is on your life it will help you **Navigate** through because it is **Necessary** for you. I pray that God continue to silence the **NOISE** in your life. Keep you under His **Shelter** so that you can **Study** His word. I pray that you continue be **SURE** that you are making the right steps. May the LORD help you receive the right **INJECTIONS** and you keep that **INTIMACY** with the father and watch Him **INCREASE** your life. Don't be **Sorry** for making the changes it help you to be open to the Lord the one that **Supplies** all of our needs. Your **Transformation** looks good on you. You where able to go through the **Test** to **Testify** the Lord is real and He is the true and living one Continue to put the **Effort** so that you can **Elevate** higher in the LORD. He wants you to keep rising up **Early** to spend time with Him. God is going to keep blessing you in **New** ways. It's the word of God that gives us **Nourishment** to get through those days that seem to be a big **Challenge** in our walk. The Lord is the best **Company** anyone can keep. He's able to **Cover** you and keep you from falling. **Yield** in to the Holy Spirit and watch God bless you through many **Years** on earth. **You** can do it with the Lord's guidance.

One thing that I've learned about being CONSISTENT with the LORD it will unlock many keys in heaven. The Lord is faithful to keeping you. If you want to redo tge Devotional its always a good and fresh start. Don't give up in walking with the LORD. I pray that your mind stays Consistency with Him. God Bless you…

Continue your journey of falling in love with the Lord. Being with Him is better than anything or anyone. When you make Him your Ruler, you won't have to worry about worldly things. He is our King, Jehovah Jireh, most of all our LORD and Savior.

Psalm 46:1-3

"God is our refuge and strength, an ever-present help in trouble. Therefore we will not fear, though the earth give way and the mountains fall into the heart of the sea, though its waters roar and foam and the mountains quake with their surging."

Isaiah 41:10

"So do not fear, for I am with you; do not be dismayed, for I am your God. I will strengthen you and help you; I will uphold you with my righteous right hand."

Philippians 4:6-7

"Do not be anxious about anything, but in every situation, by prayer and petition, with thanksgiving, present your requests to God. And the peace of God, which transcends all understanding, will guard your hearts and your minds in Christ Jesus."

Romans 8:28

Scripture to help be encouraged through life

Absolutely, here are some Bible verses that can provide encouragement through life's ups and downs:

Psalm 46:1-3

"God is our refuge and strength, an ever-present help in trouble. Therefore we will not fear, though the earth give way and the mountains fall into the heart of the sea, though its waters roar and foam and the mountains quake with their surging."

Isaiah 41:10

"So do not fear, for I am with you; do not be dismayed, for I am your God. I will strengthen you and help you; I will uphold you with my righteous right hand."

Philippians 4:6-7

"Do not be anxious about anything, but in every situation, by prayer and petition, with thanksgiving, present your requests to God. And the peace of God, which transcends all understanding, will guard your hearts and your minds in Christ Jesus."

Romans 8:28

"And we know that in all things God works for the good of those who love him, who have been called according to his purpose."

Joshua 1:9

"Have I not commanded you? Be strong and courageous. Do not be afraid; do not be discouraged, for the Lord your God will be with you wherever you go."

2 Corinthians 12:9-10

"But he said to me, 'My grace is sufficient for you, for my power is made perfect in weakness.' Therefore I will boast all the more gladly about my weaknesses, so that Christ's power may rest on me. That is why, for Christ's sake, I delight in weaknesses, in insults, in hardships, in persecutions, in difficulties. For when I am weak, then I am strong."

Psalm 55:22

"Cast your cares on the Lord and he will sustain you; he will never let the righteous be shaken."

Matthew 11:28-30

"Come to me, all you who are weary and burdened, and I will give you rest. Take my yoke upon you and learn from me, for I am gentle and humble in heart, and you will find rest for your souls. For my yoke is easy and my burden is light."

Be sure to check out other books by Whitley Witcher

- Living in the Secret Place (Psalms 91)
- Shoe Type of Women
    - (Journal to Shoe Type of Women
- Embracing the Bruise's

Made in the USA
Columbia, SC
14 January 2025